The Mysterious Mind

A consideration of consciousness, materialism & panpsychism

Eric Tiller

Vitae Publications

Copyright © 2011 by Eric Tiller

All rights reserved. This book, or parts thereof, may not be reproduced in any form without permission.

A catalogue record for this book is available from the British Library

ISBN: 978-1-907962-39-4

Published by Vitae Publications

Reading, England

For Amber

Contents

Preface 7

Introduction 9

The Mysterious Mind 11

References 107

Preface

You would be best to think of this book as having two parts. In the first part I seek to outline various well-established views concerning consciousness and the mind. In the second part I seek to outline a 'new' view concerning consciousness and the mind.

It is perhaps doubtful that there is anything truly 'new' to be said in the realm of the philosophy of mind. However, I do believe that by using different elements of some long-existing ideas, and fusing them together with some insights of my own, that a position of interest is achieved.

You would also be best to think of this book as telling a story which slowly develops. It is meant to be a fairly easy read which develops a particular view of the world. It is not meant to be a compelling and rigorous philosophical defence of a particular philosophical position.

It is more of an exploration into the unknown.

I hope that you find this exploration informative and that it provokes you into thinking about the issues for yourself.

Introduction

The mind is a truly mysterious thing. But it should be remembered that the entire universe – all parts of it – are mysterious. And it is, of course, true that the way that one conceives of the entire universe will have a major impact on how mysterious one considers the human mind to be.

In this book I consider various views concerning the nature of that most mysterious element of the mind – consciousness. Given that the nature of the universe is mysterious it is not surprising that there are various views concerning the nature and pervasiveness of consciousness.

The Mysterious Mind

I will be defending a very unpopular position – that there is the same level of consciousness in a flea as there is in me. I do not claim that this is obviously true – but simply that it is at least as intelligible as the other possibilities.

The Mysterious Mind

"The mysteries of the mind have been around for so long, and we have made so little progress on them, that the likelihood is high that some things we all tend to agree to be obvious are just not so."[1] *(Daniel Dennett)*

In this book I will be considering the possibility that there is the same level of consciousness in a flea as there is in me (or any other human). Why I am considering this possibility? I am doing so because I believe that this is a good way to explore the mysterious nature of the mind; in particular it seems a good way to explore how little we understand about both the nature of consciousness and its pervasiveness in the universe. I don't have a particular fondness for fleas, or an obsession with myself, but the comparison seems to be a useful one. The 'flea' is a representative of all relatively simple life-forms on the Earth, whilst 'me' is a representative of the complex life-form that is the human species.

As is clear from the above quote from Daniel Dennett, the fact that this possibility goes against common wisdom may actually be advantageous! I will not be claiming to have any definitive answers, but rather I will be suggesting that a range of positions on the possibility (of there being the same level of consciousness in a flea as me) are acceptable.

I start by outlining the standard definition of consciousness, and I then proceed to outline the prevailing dominant view of consciousness – materialism – the monist position which claims that consciousness can be completely explained in terms of physical brain states. Without the brain there is no consciousness. In this case there is seemingly no chance that there is the same level of consciousness in a flea as there is in me.

I then outline the arguments of Hans Jonas that consciousness is prevalent throughout the organic world. Acceptance of this position clearly entails the acceptance that consciousness is completely distinct from the brain; it also means that it precedes the brain if evolution by common descent is true.

I then suggest that if it is accepted that consciousness is prevalent throughout the organic world, then the most logical solution to the 'hard problem' of consciousness is the adoption of panpsychism. I outline how the panpsychist sees levels of consciousness within the universe, and conclude that the panpsychist undoubtedly sees a much greater level of consciousness in me than there is in a flea. I then consider the possibility that consciousness is just an illusion, and proceed to summarise the findings of the first part of the book.

In the second part of the book I propose a new paradigm called 'subvenience' which fuses together some of the positions in the first part of the book. In this paradigm there is the same level of consciousness in a flea as there is in me.

1. What is Consciousness?

"If a large number of neurons in the brain start firing in the same way, reducing the diversity of the brain's neuronal repertories, as is the case in deep sleep and epilepsy, consciousness disappears."[2] *(Edelman & Tononi)*

There is very little that we can certain about. It is often said that 'death and taxes' are certain, or that the 'sun will definitely rise tomorrow.' In reality, there is no way that we can be certain of any of these things. There is no way that we can be *certain* of death, it is possible to imagine a future where nobody pays taxes, and on occasion planets spin off their axes (which means that the 'sun might not rise'!). The only certainty seems to be that the universe contains consciousness.

Our consciousness exists within our 'material' body. An obvious conclusion to reach would be that consciousness and matter go together – they are the interior and exterior expressions of the same stuff. As Hans Jonas puts it:

> "Its [the living body] actual, concrete fullness teaches us that matter in space, otherwise experienced only from without, may have an inner horizon too and that, therefore, its extended being need not be its whole being. Seen from the only true concreteness furnished to us, both pure "extension" and pure "thought" may well appear to be mere abstractions."[3]

Yet, when we look out into the world, our typical presumption is that almost all of the stuff we are looking at contains matter but no consciousness. At the extreme are those who believe in 'solipsism.' Not only do they deny consciousness to non-human animals, plants and inanimate objects, but also to other humans. The slightly less extreme position is 'multi-brain solipsism'. This position denies consciousness to anything but a complex brain.

As the quote at the start of this section shows, there are different notions of consciousness. Edelman and Tononi claim that a human in deep sleep has no consciousness. This seems to imply that a deep sleeper is non-conscious – a zombie; this is the psychological rather than the philosophical notion of consciousness. In this book my main concern is to consider the philosophical notion of consciousness.

I will be using the following *philosophical definition of consciousness* throughout:

> 'a *state of reality* characterized by interiority, subjectivity, sentience, feeling, experience, self-agency, meaning, and purpose. Anything that has any of these has consciousness. Anything that does not would be non-conscious – blank, void, vacuous, wholly objective.'[4]

This definition can be contrasted with the psychological definition of consciousness, which refers to:

'a *state of consciousness* (e.g., awake, dreaming, joyful, fearful, mystical) above threshold awareness. It presupposes the existence of philosophical awareness.'[5]

Koch[6] identifies six categories of possible philosophical explanation for consciousness. The first two are, *consciousness depends on an immaterial soul*, and *consciousness requires behaviour*. Koch finds these unconvincing and I will not be considering them further. The third category is, *consciousness is an emergent property of biological systems*. This is the dominant materialist paradigm which I will explore in the next section. The fourth category is, *consciousness cannot be understood by scientific means*. This includes the belief that the physical brain cannot generate consciousness, which is explored in section three. The fifth category is, *consciousness requires fundamentally new laws*. This includes panpsychism which I will be exploring in sections four and five. The final category is *consciousness is illusory*. I explore this paradigm in section six.

2. The Materialism Paradigm

"Materialists...insist that there is no "consciousness" substance separate from a "brain substance.""[7] *(Edelman & Tononi)*

The dominant materialist/physicalist paradigm holds that consciousness is produced by the brain. According to this view there is just one substance pervading the universe: the physical. Koch states that, "consciousness emerges from neuronal features of the brain. Understanding the material basis of consciousness is unlikely to require and exotic new physics, but rather a much deeper appreciation of how highly interconnected networks of a large number of heterogeneous neurons work."[8]

According to this view consciousness is clearly restricted to organisms with brains – as is clear from the quote at the start of the section – and is usually restricted to organisms with large brains and / or a high level of encephalization (the ratio of brain weight to body weight). Koch states that, "It is plausible that some species of animals – mammals in particular – possess some, but not necessarily all, of the features of consciousness; that they see, smell, and otherwise experience the world."[9]

The materialist thus allows that animals such as chimpanzees and dolphins have consciousness, and that the consciousness in them is not totally incomparable to the level of consciousness in a human. However, they clearly restrict consciousness to a small privileged band of animals, and see a sliding scale of consciousness within these animals – a scale with humans at a far-removed apex. The materialists would find the notion that there could be the same level of consciousness in a flea as in me as utterly preposterous.

Following the work of Charles Darwin and Alfred Wallace, the materialists claim that their position is reinforced by the evolutionary perspective. Consciousness is supposedly something that has arisen in the evolution of complexity. They argue that there has been a tandem evolution of consciousness and brain due to the evolutionary survival requirement of information processing. Ervin Laszlo describes the materialist position as follows:

> "as organisms become more complex, they require a more complex "computer" to steer them so they can get the food, the mate, and the related resources they need in order to survive and reproduce. At a given point in this devel-

opment, consciousness appears. Synchronized neural firings and transmission of energy and chemical substances between synapses produce the qualitative stream of experience that makes up our consciousness."[10]

There is a weaker version of the materialist paradigm which relates to the nervous system rather than the brain. Koch states that, "At present it is unknown to what extent conscious perception is common to *all* animals. It is probable that consciousness correlates to some extent with the complexity of the organism's nervous system. Squids, bees, fruit flies, and even roundworms are all capable of fairly sophisticated behaviours. Perhaps they too possess some level of awareness;

perhaps they too can feel pain, experience pleasure, and see."[11] On this weak interpretation consciousness is the sole preserve of the animal world. Later in the book I will be claiming that this division between entities which have brains and nervous systems, and those which don't, is of some importance.

3. The Separation of Consciousness from Brain

"life presents itself as an ascending scale in which are placed the sophistications of form, the lure of sense and the spur of desire, the

command of limb and powers to act, the reflection of consciousness and the reach for truth." [12] *(Hans Jonas)*

Hans Jonas in *The Phenomenon of Life* argues for an existential interpretation of biological facts to support his belief that mind is prefigured throughout organic existence. His view is that, "scientific biology, by its rules confined to the physical, outward facts, must ignore the dimension of inwardness that belongs to life: in so doing, it submerges the distinction of "animate" and "inanimate." A new reading of the biological record may recover the inner-dimension – that which we know best – for the understanding of things organic and so reclaim for the psycho-physical unity of life that place in the theoretical scheme which it had lost through the divorce of the material and mental since Descartes."[13]

Jonas, as is clear from the quote at the start of this section, thinks that consciousness is prevalent throughout the organic world. This means that the vast majority of planetary organisms have consciousness without an associated brain. In Jonas's view there is thus a clear separation between consciousness and brain. If we also accept Darwin's notion of evolution by common descent, then it is clear that consciousness preceded the brain, and is more ontologically fundamental than the brain.

In evolutionary terms Jonas sees freedom as arising with the emergence of metabolism on the early Earth, "it is in the dark stirrings of primeval organic substance that a principle of freedom shines forth for the first time within the vast necessity of the physical universe."[14] The origin of planetary life is thus the origination of freedom, it also entails pervasive consciousness. However, there were no brains around at this time. Therefore, accepting the arguments of Jonas leads to the rejection of the physicalist paradigm (which holds that brains are the only part of the universe which generate consciousness).

Christian de Quincey argues that, "If we assume that consciousness depends on activity in the brain, or must always be associated with brain events, then we should be aware that we are ruling out the option of extracerebral consciousness or experience, such as whole-body consciousness, or cellular consciousness."[15] Laszlo expresses similar sentiments when he claims that, "what we call "matter" is the aspect we apprehend when we look at a person, a plant, or a molecule from the *outside*; "mind" is the readout we get when we look at the same thing from the *inside*."[16]

4. The Hard Problem of Consciousness

"the concept of freedom can indeed guide us like Ariadne's thread through the interpretation of life. As to the mystery of origins – it is closed to us. Most persuasive to me is the hypothesis that even the transition from inanimate to animate

> *substance, the first feat of matter's organising itself for life, was actuated by a tendency in the depth of being toward the very modes of freedom to which this transition opened the gate. Such a hypothesis affects the entire inorganic substrate on which the structure of freedom is reared."*[17] *(Hans Jonas)*

If Jonas's argument that consciousness is prevalent throughout the organic world is accepted then it follows that there is consciousness in both a flea and me. The next question that needs to be addressed is the 'hard problem' of consciousness. A universe without consciousness is conceivable; the 'hard problem' – a term originated by David Chalmers – is the question of why consciousness exists. Consciousness exists now, so the question has to be asked if it emerged at some stage in the past. Accepting that consciousness *is* prevalent throughout the organic world shifts the question of emergence to the origins of planetary life. Does consciousness emerge with the origination of planetary life? Or does consciousness pervade the inorganic as well as the organic world?

If it is hypothesised that the organic world has consciousness but the inorganic world does not, then this raises the question as to how it is possible that consciousness could arise out of completely unconscious matter on the early Earth. If it is hypothesised that it is impossible for consciousness to emerge out of matter that is utterly unconscious, then the hard problem dissipates into a non-problem. It would be accepted that every physical thing has consciousness, and the panpsychism paradigm would therefore be accepted.

The viewpoint of Jonas on the 'hard problem' is quoted at the start of this section. His favoured solution is clearly that there is a drive toward freedom emanating from the inanimate world. However, the problem is not of direct concern to him. Following the quote at the start of this section he states that, "For our purpose we need not commit ourselves to this or any hypothesis on first origins, for where we start, the "first strivings" have long occurred."[18] We can therefore surmise that Jonas himself favours the panpsychist solution that the 'hard problem' is a non-problem – his inanimate drive towards freedom signifies the presence of consciousness in the inanimate. However, he decides not to tackle the 'hard problem' himself.

The traditional home of the 'hard problem' is the brain. However, following Jonas the problem can be fruitfully repositioned to the emergence of planetary life. This repositioning entails that the claim of the materialist that brains give rise to consciousness due to the evolutionary need for bigger brains and greater information processing capacities is to be rejected. In response to this proposed repositioning the materialist either has to reject the arguments of Jonas, or come up with another story to explain consciousness in a physically monistic world. It seems likely a new story would be significantly less believable than their current story; so a rejection is the most likely response. If the repositioning is accepted this significantly bolsters the likelihood of panpsychism.

Colin McGinn asks, "How could the aggregation of millions of individually insentient neurons generate subjective awareness?...Somehow, we feel, the water of the physical brain is turned into the wine of consciousness, but we draw a total blank on the nature of this conversion."[19] Clearly, the repositioning of this question from the brain to the emergence of planetary life makes the water into wine conversion *even more miraculous*. However, since there are good reasons to make the repositioning the appropriate conclusion seems to be to favour panpsychism (rather than retreat to materialism).

Christian de Quincey argues that materialism, dualism and idealism are inadequate ontologies for a science of consciousness, whilst panpsychism provides a coherent foundation. He criticises the materialists for their belief that subjective mind could appear out of a wholly objective reality. He argues that, "Such emergence would require an inexplicable ontological jump – a miracle. *In a purely physical world, the appearance of mind would be a supernatural event.*"[20] He criticises the dualists because he believes that, "there is no conceivable way that *unextended*, ghostlike mind could ever exert an influence or cause an effect on solid, weighty, extended matter... Dualism requires the intervention of a miracle."[21]

He also criticises idealism because the absolute idealists believe matter is merely an illusion, and "we just don't live as though matter is an illusion,"[22] and the emanationist idealists for believing that matter could possible emanate from spirit, which, "would amount to a miracle of producing something physical from wholly non-physical being."[23] Materialism, dualism and idealism thus all require their own individual miraculous occurrences, whilst panpsychism requires no such miracle. With particular reference to the 'hard problem', de Quincey argues that, *"It is inconceivable that sentience (subjectivity, consciousness), could ever emerge or evolve from wholly insentient (objective, physical) matter."*[24]

Laszlo argues that, "We do not need to explain how unconscious matter generates immaterial consciousness, because matter is not entirely unconscious, nor is consciousness fully divorced from matter...David Chalmers's "hard" problem evaporates."[25]

So, many people believe that it is highly improbable, if not impossible, that on the early Earth the origination of life entailed the transformation of unconscious matter into conscious organisms. For these people the most logical conclusion to reach is that the origination of life was *the emergence of a higher level of consciousness out of a lower level of consciousness*. There is no need to create problems and mysteries where none exist.

David Chalmers argues that, "If we want to take consciousness seriously, we must admit phenomenal or protophenomenal properties as fundamental."[26] He claims that, "we ought to take the possibility of panpsychism seriously: there seem to be no knockdown arguments against the view, and there are various positive reasons why one might embrace it."[27] I will do just this in the next section.

5. The Panpsychism Paradigm

"a single cell could be conscious, not to mention molecules, atoms, and elementary particles."[28] *(Christian de Quincey)*

"the idea that the fundamental contrast between organic and inorganic lies not in the constitution of the object but in the attitude of the observer is well worth considering."[29] *(Erwin Schrodinger)*

Panpsychism is a form of 'dualistic-monism.' De Quincey describes panpsychism as, "a cosmological and ontological theory that proposes all objective bodies (objects) in the universe, including those we usually classify as "inanimate," possess an interior, subjective reality (they are also subjects). In other words, there is something it feels like from within to be a body (of any kind)."[30]

De Quincey draws a distinction between Leibnizian panpsychism in which there are both individuals *and* aggregates, and Pantheistic panpsychism. In Leibnizian panpsychism, "all individuals and holistic systems of monads (organisms) have experience, aggregates as such (e.g., rocks, clouds or oceans) do not have experience (though their individual constituents do)."[31] In Pantheistic panpsychism all entities, that is, both aggregates and individuals, have experience. A rock is thus not just a collection of individual conscious constituents; there is a greater consciousness at the level of the whole object.

Panpsychism is clearly a very minority position compared to the dominant contemporary physicalist paradigm. However, even the panpsychists reject the notion that there could be the same level of consciousness in a flea as in me. They see an immensely small – bordering on negligible – level of consciousness in the inanimate world. Moving into the animate world they see a sliding scale of consciousness throughout the living world. Plants and trees are 'individuals' which have a fairly low level of 'emergent consciousness'; the invertebrates and lower animals have a higher level of 'emergent consciousness'; mammals have a higher level still, and humans are at the apex. It is thus the panpsychist belief that the consciousness levels of two 'individuals' as diverse as a human and a flea are quite different.

In fact, panpsychists are at pains to stress their belief in vastly different levels of consciousness between entities. As de Quincey describes it:

"Too often, the knee-jerk response to panpsychism has been the retort that it implies atoms, molecules, or cells, as well as plants and rocks, experience an interior psychic life with all the *conscious richness* of human desires, fears, evaluations, thoughts, choices and dreams.

Such a vision of nature would indeed be exaggerated projection and absurd anthropomorphism. But just as a dog or chimpanzee can have experiences that differ from human consciousness, so too lizards, worms, bacteria, atoms, and electrons may each have their own characteristic, species-specific forms of experience – *primitive feelings* that respond to their particular environmental stimuli."[32]

David Chalmers in *The Conscious Mind* argues for a variety of panpsychism that is grounded in what he calls 'naturalistic dualism'. He argues that it is impossible that physical facts could entail the facts about consciousness, which means that natural supervenience exists rather than logical supervenience. His version of panpsychism entails a *principle of organizational invariance* which means that, "A given functional organization can be realized by diverse physical systems. For example, the organization realized by the brain at the neural level might in principle be realized by a silicon system."[33] He stresses that conscious experiences arise due to supervenience in accordance with the complexity of functional organization, with: "very simple systems having very simple phenomenology, and complex systems having complex phenomenology."[34]

The Mysterious Mind

Panexperientialism and Protophenomenalism

The terms panexperientialism (David Ray Griffin) and protophenomenalism (David Chalmers) are also used to emphasize the differences in 'consciousness' between entities. Griffin[35] claims that lower entities may only have experience rather than genuine consciousness. However, this is just panpsychism according to the definition of consciousness I have outlined, because experience qualifies as being philosophically conscious.

Chalmers notion of protophenomenalism is slightly different because he argues that, "the mere instantiation of such a [protophenomenal] quality does not entail experience, but instantiation of numerous such properties could do so jointly."[36] He admits that, "it is hard to imagine how this could work (we know that it cannot work for standard physical properties),"[37] but he doesn't think that it can be ruled out *a priori*. I would also have to agree that it is hard to imagine how it could work – it clearly requires the water into wine miracle that was described in the last section. Protophenomenalism should thus be rejected. Chalmers simply offers it as an unlikely possible alternative to his favoured view of phenomenalism. Having considered panexperientialism (which is panpsychism) and protophenomenalism (which we have rejected) we can return to our consideration of panpsychism.

The panpsychist belief can be summed up as, "different qualities of experience and consciousness evolve and *emerge* at different levels of complexity."[38] Laszlo has coined the term 'evolutionary panpsychism' to make this abundantly clear. He argues that the term stresses that panpsychists do *not* claim that, "psyche is present throughout reality in the same way, at the same level of development. We say that psyche evolves, the same as matter."[39]

6. The Illusion of Consciousness

"We're all zombies. Nobody is conscious – not in the systematically mysterious way that supports such doctrines as epiphenomenalism! I can't prove that no such sort of consciousness exists. I also cannot prove that gremlins don't exist. The

best I can do is show that there is no respectable motivation for believing in it."[40] *(Daniel Dennett)*

In *Consciousness Explained* Daniel Dennett argues that consciousness – as is usually conceptualized – is just an elaborate illusion. The illusion is generated by the interactions of the senses with motor output, and is reinforced by learning. In his account subjective feelings and qualia have no basis in reality; subjectivity is an elaborate illusion. He claims that he explains, "the various phenomena that compose what we call consciousness, showing how they are all physical effects of the brain's activities, how these activities evolved, and how they give rise to illusions about their own powers and properties."[41]

Dennett argues against what he calls the Cartesian Theatre – a central headquarters in the brain which is the unique location for a single "stream of consciousness." Instead he outlines what he calls a Multiple Drafts model, according to which, "all varieties of perception – indeed, all varieties of thought or mental activity – are accompanied in the brain by parallel, multitrack processes of interpretation and elaboration of sensory inputs. Information entering the nervous system is under continuous "editorial revision.""[42]

The phenomena of human consciousness can thus be explained, "in terms of the operations of a "virtual machine," a sort of evolved (and evolving) computer program that shapes the activities of the brain. There is no Cartesian Theatre; there are just

Multiple Drafts composed by processes of content fixation playing various semi-independent roles in the brain's larger economy of controlling a human body's journey through life."[43] He calls this "virtual machine" the Joycean Machine.

Dennett argues that, "Thousands of memes, mostly borne by language, but also by wordless "images" and other data structures, take up residence in an individual brain, shaping its tendencies and thereby turning it into a mind."[44] This is clearly a functionalist vision as, "Anyone or anything that has such a virtual machine as its control system is conscious because it has such a virtual machine."[45] He is thus willing to accept that, "If consciousness is something over and above the Joycean machine, I have not yet provided a theory of consciousness at all, even if other puzzling questions have been answered."[46]

He claims to have undermined the presumption that there are, ""intrinsic" properties – qualia – that constitute *what it is like* to have one conscious experience or another."[47] He supports, "the "reductionist" path of *identifying* "the way it is with me" with the sum total of all the idiosyncratic reactive dispositions inherent in my nervous system as a result of my being confronted by a certain pattern of stimulation."[48]

7. A Summary of the Previous Sections

"The limits of our minds are just not the limits of reality. It is deplorably anthropocentric to insist that reality be constrained by what the human mind can conceive."[49] (Colin McGinn)

I have reviewed four different possible philosophical explanations for consciousness. They seem to fall nicely into two groups; materialism and Dennett on the one hand, and Jonas and panpsychism on the other. Both of these routes are acceptable routes of enquiry. The repositioning of the 'hard problem' at the emergence of planetary life, when combined with the 'water into wine' argument, forms a strong case for panpsychism. In addition, Dennett also makes a good argument regarding the evolution of the brain and the elaborate illusions that it generates. However, I am unconvinced by certain aspects of both panpsychism and Dennett's position.

I do not agree with Dennett that, "Since there hasn't always been human consciousness, it has to have arisen from prior phenomena that *weren't* instances of consciousness."[50] We have seen from our analysis in sections three and four that this isn't necessarily so. I also take issue with the panpsychist belief in emergence, differential consciousness levels and Chalmers organizational invariance (I also reject Dennett's functionalism).

I am now going to outline a new view of consciousness that entails the fusing together of the opposing positions of panpsychism and Dennett, and which loses the unconvincing aspects of both. In the following sections I outline the four core premises of the theory – which I call 'subvenience.' Premise 1 is *the fallacy of levels*. Premise 2 is *the spectre of non-emergence*. Premise 3 is *the continuous flux of object boundaries*. Premise 4 is *the inauthenticity of illusion*. 'Subvenience' preserves the best bits of Dennett and panpsychism, loses the worst, and fuses them together in the process.

My starting assumption is the panpsychist belief in atomic consciousness. This starting point obviously implies that there is consciousness in both me and a flea. In the following sections I first present premises which lead to the conclusion that I do not have a higher level of consciousness than a flea. I then suggest that my experience of the world is much more inauthentic than that of a flea.

8. The Fallacy of Levels

"Human beings have simply assumed that they were the most intelligent and have then looked for the morphological support for that assumption. But the assumption itself may be wrong."[51] *(Fichtelius and Sjolander)*

If one agrees with the arguments forwarded by Jonas regarding all of life being conscious, then it follows that consciousness is more ontologically fundamental than the brain. This means that there is no reason to expect a direct link between brain size / composition and the level of consciousness experienced by the organism. We can therefore conclude that an organism with a large brain cannot be said to be more 'conscious' than an organism with a small brain.

Thomas Nagel famously asked what it would be like to be a bat. He claimed that, "an organism has conscious mental states if and only if there is something that it is like for the organism."[52] For Nagel there *is* something that it is like to be a bat, but we cannot possibly imagine what it is. He states that, "we believe that bats feel some versions of pain, fear, hunger, and lust...But we believe that these experiences also have in each case a specific subjective character, which it is beyond our ability to conceive."[53] This is the key point. There is an immense variation in subjectivity between organisms, and because this variability is beyond our ability to conceive, it is impossible to say whether a particular subjective experience is at a higher level of consciousness than another.

Nagel sees consciousness as fundamentally connected with a *point of view*, an outlook which constitutes a limitation upon what is conceivable. He states that, "If physicalism is to be defended, the phenomenological features must themselves be given a physical account. But when we examine their subjective character it seems that such a result is impossible. The reason is that every subjective phenomenon is essentially connected with a single point of view, and it seems inevitable that an objective, physical theory will abandon that point of view."[54] If every atom is conscious then in a sense every atom has 'a point of view'. 'Subvenists' accept this notion, but they also claim that animals with nervous systems / brains also have a 'point of view' in a different sense; this will be explored in *Section 11*.

It is easy to see why the attempt to ascribe a level of consciousness to another entity is hopelessly doomed. This is because if a higher level of consciousness exists in some non-human entities (which live on the Earth) than exists in humans –

which seems very possible given the vast periods of time many entities have been around compared to the minimal duration of human existence – then we would not know. This is a recasting of the old philosophical problem that *only the cleverest person on the planet can realise that they are the cleverest;* other people may think that they are cleverer, but the cleverest person is so clever that he could be tricking them into believing this. In my recast scenario the participants are not human beings but *non-human entities*. We may think that we are at the apex of consciousness and cleverness – but there is no possible way that we could ever be sure of such an assertion.

Just as we, as adult humans, instinctively help those who we consider less conscious and able than ourselves, such as our newborn, or our pets when they are in distress or danger, other species may do the same for us. They, out of compassion for humans of a lower consciousness, may come to our rescue when in mortal danger. In fact, this has been documented on numerous occasions with respect to dolphins. Studies of dolphins and *Homo sapiens* have in fact resulted in the claim that, "The surprising conclusion of this comparison is that the dolphin brain *could* be superior to ours."[55] From the perspectives of materialism and panpsychism this would suggest that dolphin consciousness exceeds human consciousness. From the 'subvenience' perspective this debate is obviously a non-issue because of the belief in *the fallacy of levels* (dolphins and humans have the same level of consciousness – however, from the 'subvenience perspective' there could still be different levels of intelligence).

9. The Spectre of Non-Emergence

"The problem of emergence has a long history in philosophy, and is particularly relevant to philosophy of mind...Only dualists can avoid the issue of emergence altogether because for them mind belongs in a completely different ontological domain."[56] (Christian de Quincey)

In this book, I have followed Koch, and have considered dualism sufficiently unlikely to be considered.

It thus seems to follow from the above quote that I am tied to the notion of the emergence of consciousness. Both materialism and panpsychism each have their own hypothesized stories to explain the emergence of consciousness. I am going to suggest that it is perfectly acceptable to reject both dualism and emergence.

Panpsychists stress that there is a sliding scale of consciousness throughout the animate and inanimate world. They see consciousness in 'individuals' as something that *emerges* out of the lesser psychic entities that comprise an 'individual' (in Pantheistic panpsychism this *emergence* also occurs in 'aggregates'). There are thus varying levels of 'emergent consciousness' within organisms which are directly correlated to the functional complexity of the organism. Panpsychists argue that there *is* an incomparably higher level of consciousness in me than a flea due to the differential 'emergence' rates between the flea and me.

The question of the 'emergence' of consciousness is absolutely crucial. This is because in panpsychism there is atomic consciousness within organisms. Therefore, in the 'pre-emergence' state it inevitably follows that there could be the same level of consciousness in a flea as in me. This is because either atomic consciousness is at a fixed level, in which case there would be the same level of consciousness in a flea and me, or there is variable atomic consciousness, in which case there will most certainly be fleas with a higher level of consciousness within them than in me. The question of 'emergence' is therefore central to consciousness; without it all entities would have the same consciousness (I am going to assume, in the rest of the book, that atomic consciousness levels are 'fixed'. Of course, if they are in fact 'variable', then this would further *strengthen* the position I am outlining).

The belief in the 'emergence' of consciousness has no evidence to support it. It seems to have been invented for anthropocentric reasons – to justify the human perception of 'superior consciousness'; this is clear from the quote at the beginning of section eight. The 'emergence' of consciousness is magical, mythical and mysterious, and it is totally unobservable. There seems to be no reason to hypothesize such an occurrence – to create such an invention.

'Subvenience' totally rejects the notion of emergence, and holds that there are fixed consciousness levels within entities. It can thus also be referred to as the 'Variable Expression of Fixed Consciousness Paradigm'. The claim is that the maximum level of attainable consciousness has been in existence since the beginning of the universe. It is *not* something that emerges in any sense of the word. All objects – from stones, to trees, to fleas, to peas, to cheese, to John Cleese – have inside them the same fixed level of consciousness. 'Subvenists' refer to the atomic consciousness currently present in any entity as its 'subvenience base'. The only difference between entities is not the consciousness within them, but, the way that their consciousness results in 'variable organismic experiences'. Different entities will have different experiences of the consciousness within. This is *the spectre of non-emergence.*

10. The Continuous Flux of Object Boundaries

"Whilst there is nothing that it is like to be a brick, or an ink-jet printer, there is, presumably, something that it is like to be a bat, or a dolphin; and there is certainly something that it is like to be a human being."[57]   *(Davies & Humphreys)*

Materialists and Panpsychists believe that there are distinct objects which are the home of a given level of consciousness. A human is a distinct object with a high level of consciousness, and a flea is a distinct object with a low level of consciousness. In contrast, 'subvenists' argue that there is no such thing as a distinct object. Every nano-second object boundaries are in flux.

Leibnizian panpsychists argue that there is consciousness in a brick; however, they do not believe that there is something specifically that it is like to be a brick. In contrast, Pantheistic panpsychists argue that there is something that it is like to be a brick – they believe in emergence in 'aggregates' as well as in 'individuals.' 'Subvenience' transcends these two positions by stressing that whilst there is something that it feels like to be every entity – even a brick – there is no distinct feeling of 'brickness.'

The existence of a distinct feeling within a brick is simply the result of the length of time that the occupying atoms have been cohabiting the same spatial location.

The defining factor in isolating the consciousness of a brick is that its constitutive atoms have a distinct spatio-temporal embeddedness. The same atoms are embedded together in the same spatio-temporal location for a certain length of time. The longer is the period of spatio-temporal embeddedness of a given group of atoms the greater will be the distinctive consciousness of the resulting object. This is in fact the definition of an object. Definitions based on functionality are anthropocentric inventions that clearly aid our day-to-day lives, but which just as clearly have no ontological reality.

So, the consciousness of an average brick is far more pronounced than that of a raindrop; that of an ancient forest is more distinctive than that of a recently planted forest. It is not the case that a lengthened period of spatio-temporal embeddedness increases the level of consciousness; it simply makes the entity more distinct from all the surrounding entities in the universe.

A few simple thought experiments should make it clear why in reality there are *no fixed boundaries* that separate any entity from any other entity; why there are solely spatial and temporal relations. Imagine a stone that is in a field. It must have been in existence for a given length of time. The conscious atoms that currently comprise the 'object' will thus have been spatio-temporally embedded together for a given duration of time. The atoms will also have become embedded with the atoms in the grass on which they lie; however, as the spatio-temporal embeddedness of the atoms within the stone is greater than the spatio-temporal duration of the atoms of the 'stone plus grass,' this distinguishes them as 'objects'. However, the longer they are in contact the more they become embedded, and the less they are distinct entities.

Further imagine what would happen if we were to cut the stone into two and take half of the stone to an adjacent field. In this scenario the two halves would still be 'connected' to each other due to their period of spatio-temporal embeddedness; there is, in fact, a perfect positive correlation between duration and connection. However, as time passes, the two halves, whilst retaining their connections, will become more distinct from each other as 'objects'. Furthermore, the half of the original stone that was removed will also become more distinct from the grass in the former field, and will gradually become more embedded with the grass in the new field.

A more vivid case would be that of a soldier who loses his leg. Imagine he loses his leg and then gets flown home to the other side of the world. The long period of spatio-temporal embeddedness between his leg and the rest of his body, would mean that there are still connections between them; in a sense they are still part of the same 'object' despite their short period of separation. If someone on the battlefield shoots his leg, we shouldn't be surprised if the soldier feels pain in what he might describe as his 'phantom limb'.

These kinds of effects have been detected by Cleve Backster. His experiments with pure cell cultures derived from the white mouth cells of subjects reveals the effects of spatio-temporal embeddedness. In one such test, "a former Navy gunner who was at Pearl Harbor during the Japanese attack was shown a TV program depicting the attack. He showed no particular reaction until the face of a Navy gunner appeared on the screen, followed by a shot of a Japanese plane falling into the sea. At that moment the needle of the lie detector attached to his cells twelve kilometres away jumped."[58] The distant cells were reacting to his strong emotional response.

In conclusion, a brick can be thought of as a congregation of conscious atoms that is involved in a continuous flux with its surroundings. If it is moved continuously from place to place it will be a fairly distinct object. However, if it is part of a very old house then it will be barely a different object from the surrounding bricks in the wall. In reality, there are porous and continuously changing boundaries between what we define as 'objects' for ease of anthropocentric understanding. There are no completely distinct *anythings*.

11. The Inauthenticity of Illusion

"the self is not a proper physical part of an organism or a brain, but...an abstraction."[59] *(Daniel Dennett)*

I have so far outlined the 'subvenience' position concerning the lack of differences in consciousness levels between entities, the non-emergence of atomic consciousness, and the fluidity of boundaries between 'objects' which enables consciousness to move between 'objects'. These jointly entail the conclusion that there is the same level of consciousness in a flea as there is in me. It is atoms that feel and experience the world and not organisms.

However, there are surely differences between being a human and being a flea. If these differences are not in consciousness, what are they? For 'subvenists' the differences can be described as *the inauthenticity of illusion*.

In 'subvenience' there is no fundamental difference between the animate and the inanimate world. However, it is believed that there is an important difference between animals that have nervous systems and brains on the one hand, and those plants, 'inanimate' objects and few lower animals, on the other, that do not. All entities have a spatio-temporal 'subvenience base'. However, the presence of a brain or a nervous system creates an 'illusory organismic superstructure' which is the result of the 'subvening' (which can be thought of as 'underlaying' or 'underpinning') of the nervous system / brain by the atomic consciousness of the 'subvenience base'. This 'illusory organismic superstructure' is what gives rise to 'variable organismic experiences'. These experiences vary between every entity that has a brain or a nervous system, because it is linked with a unique 'subvenience base' – no two bases can ever be the same. This means that no two entities can ever have identical experiences (this is clearly incompatible with functionalism).

To reiterate, in 'subvenience' the atomic consciousness in an entity forms a 'subvenience base' on which a nervous system or brain can supervene. It is in this process of 'brain supervenience' that an 'illusory organismic superstructure' is created. Qualia are the domain of the 'subvenience base'; they occur in all animate and inanimate entities because all entities contain conscious atoms. Variations in experiences above this base level are illusions resulting from 'nervous system / brain supervenience'. This notion is of course almost an inversion of the traditional conception of the 'mind' supervening on the brain.

It is clear that an organism with a basic nervous system will only have a small 'illusory organismic superstructure', whilst an organism with a large brain will have a larger superstructure. Therefore, an organism with a big brain and a high encephalization rate will have a much more complex 'illusory organismic superstructure' than a flea, but both will have the same level of consciousness within them.

This is the point where Daniel Dennett makes his entrance into the 'subvenience' paradigm. There is a connection between the postulated 'illusory organismic superstructure' and the arguments of Dennett that consciousness is an illusion. In the 'subvenience' paradigm there are illusory experiences created by the nervous system / brain as it supervenes on the fixed consciousness present in the organism. In Dennett's account there are just illusory experiences. 'Subvenists' thus accept most of Dennett's account, as this supports their view that what humans think they experience as the 'apex' of consciousness is just an elaborate illusion. However, for 'subvenists' *all* brains and all nervous systems entail such an illusion.

However, in contrast to Dennett, 'subvenists' do believe qualia occur in humans, because they believe that humans have a fixed level of consciousness within them that 'subvenes' the brain. The 'subvenience base' of atomic consciousness is the home of qualia. It follows that for 'subvenists' qualia occur in all animate and inanimate entities – as they all contain this same level of fixed consciousness. It is only in animals that qualia are accompanied by illusions of varying complexity that are directly related to the functional complexity of the nervous system and the brain.

A high encephalization rate therefore leads to a high level of illusions – there will be a sliding scale of illusion throughout the animal world that varies with functional complexity. This is *the inauthentic-*

ity of illusion. Inanimate entities and plants experience pure consciousness (there are no illusions within them). The vast majority of animals are severed from pure consciousness by their varying illusions. Humans are close to the apex of inauthenticity.

12. 'Subvenience' – the New Paradigm

"The world is...a vast causal network of phenomenal properties underlying the physical laws that science postulates."[60] *(David Chalmers)*

In the 'subvenience' paradigm what we usually think of as our consciousness is largely an elaborate illusion, a similar illusion to the one argued for by Dennett. Real consciousness is located in the atomic 'subvenience base' which is located in all entities. This base interacts with the nervous system in any organism that has one thereby creating illusions within the organism that aid its survival. It is the presence of atomic consciousness that enables all entities to experience genuine and unique qualia. The subjective qualia are not a function of the brain, but simply of atomic consciousness. It has been suggested that differences between organisms are in the realm of individual variation in organismic experiences, rather than between different levels of consciousness. It follows that my experience is no doubt very different from that of a flea, but that there is no reason to attribute to me a higher level of consciousness – I just have a more complex matrix of illusions.

The fixed atomic consciousness can be thought of as being 'revealed' or given 'variable expression' within different entities – due to atomic composition and form. Every entity will have a *unique atomic composition* because all atoms contain *different* consciousness, meaning that the overall consciousness within every entity is different. The *form* of the actual entity only plays a role in organisms with nervous systems. This is because the concept of distinct objects with differing functionality is an anthropogenic construction; in reality there are just differing spatio-temporal relations between conscious atoms. However, organisms with nervous systems have a unique 'illusory organismic superstructure' which gives rise to unique experiences for the organism. All other entities are part of the 'universal subvenience base' of atomic consciousness.

'Unique organismic experiences' are clearly not the same as the 'emergence' of consciousness within an entity that occurs in panpsychism. There is no emergence of consciousness in either 'individuals' or 'aggregates;' the conscious whole is not more than the sum of the conscious parts. The conscious whole simply is the parts. Entities with a nervous system have an additional 'illusory organismic superstructure.'

Human consciousness is therefore simply the result of the fact that the universe is composed of stuff that is conscious. It always has been – nothing has emerged. The human illusion of greater consciousness is due to the nature of our 'variable expression' – the information-processing abilities of our brain are subvened superstructural experiences that have evolved to aid survival. Human consciousness is not a unique apex; it is simply a transitory home.

When an entity loses some of its constitutive atoms, or the whole entity dies (if the entity is 'living'), then the conscious atoms will re-emerge in another entity. From this perspective 'subvenience' gives us a completely new perspective from which to view the rest of nature. If a fixed consciousness resides in atoms and is given variable expression via the stuff in which it currently resides, then a holistic approach is appropriate. The consciousness in humans today would be a different expression of the same consciousness that previously found expression in such diverse things as dinosaurs, stones and ancient forests. Furthermore, the consciousness expressed through contemporary vivisection subjects would be the same as that which was expressed in some of our human ancestors. The only difference being the level of expression enabled by the functional complexity of the entity currently resided in.

Due to the strength of the physicalist paradigm we are used to thinking about this biogeochemical cycling in terms of matter only - the elements such as carbon, phosphorous and sulphur are simply dead materials cycling around the planet and through our bodies. However, when atomic consciousness is brought into the picture this recognised cycling of the biogeochemical elements that comprise our bodies takes on a whole new meaning. 'My' consciousness would have a long history, residing in a whole plethora of both animate and inanimate objects throughout history and into the distant future. However, it should be remembered that 'my' consciousness just refers to a multitude of conscious atoms that reside in my body for differential durations; there is no 'conscious me'.

The fact that animals have an 'illusory organismic superstructure' makes it easier to imagine what it would be like to be an animal rather than a non-animal. Given our experience of consciousness we intuitively assume that a predicate for consciousness is the freedom of movement – to be able to engage in behaviour. This is why we find it hard to imagine being an inanimate entity. This intuition is partially correct – it only makes sense trying to imagine being an entity with a nervous system, because these are the only entities with which are creators of a 'world' through an 'illusory organismic superstructure'.

It is futile trying to imagine what it would be like to be an entity without a nervous system. The inanimate world and the plant world due to their lack of 'illusory organismic superstructures' effectively constitute one massive 'subvenience base' of conscious atoms, which are in a constant state of flux between 'object' boundaries. Furthermore, the concept of individual 'objects' with separate functions has no ontological basis, but is simply a result of human language. It is out of this massive 'subvenience base' that organisms with nervous systems have evolved which have unique experiences. There is thus something that it is like to be a bat, whilst there is surely nothing that it is like to be a battery. A battery will have uniqueness as a result of its spatio-temporal embeddedness; however, it is purely composed of the universal 'subvenience base'. There is no unique quality of 'battery-ness'. The quality of 'bat-ness' is a result of the fact that bats have 'illusory organismic superstructures.' However, there is no difference in consciousness between bats and batteries; the spatio-temporally embedded consciousness in a battery can 'feel.'

Chalmers argues that there is something that it is like to be any information-processing system; he claims that it will "certainly not be very interesting to be a thermostat."[61] 'Subvenists' reject this idea. For them a thermostat is simply a collection of conscious atoms that is part of the 'universal subvenience base'. Attributing a thermostat a special phenomenal quality of 'thermostat-ness' is unwarranted. The only qualities are those of the spatio-temporally embedded constitutive atoms. Humans *cannot* create consciousness, because we cannot create atoms – we can only change matter from one form to another; the Earth and the Universe are 'closed systems' with regards to matter. All we can do is create complex robots which have the illusion of consciousness.

For the 'subvenist' consciousness does *not* evolve over time. However, it is accepted that the organization of matter *does* evolve over time. Given that consciousness and matter are two aspects of the same stuff, the logical conclusion is that the unchanging consciousness is responsible for the evolving matter. Chalmers alludes to this possibility in the quote at the start of this section by proposing that phenomenal properties underlie physical laws.

13. Summary and Objections

A brief summary of the arguments presented, along with some of the objections to 'subvenience', are considered in the following dialogue between *Fleabus*, who as a 'subvenist' thinks fleas have the same level of consciousness as humans, and *Jim*, who is a sceptic.

Fleabus: Jim, I propose that you are no more conscious than a flea!

Jim: How absurd!

Fleabus: I can try and convince you.

Jim: Do you really believe that a flea could have the same level of consciousness as me?

Fleabus: Yes. It follows from accepting the separation of consciousness from brain, and the most logical solution to the 'hard problem' – panpsychism.

Jim: But, if I choose not to accept such things?

Fleabus: Then you most certainly would be more conscious than a flea! But the arguments for such things are not ridiculous.

The Mysterious Mind

Jim: But even if I do accept such things, surely I can still believe that I am more conscious than a flea?

Fleabus: You can indeed if you are a panpsychist. For them the same levels of inherent consciousness give rise to differential emergence with functional complexity.

Jim: So in reality I *am* more conscious than a flea – your arguments are just technical mumbo-jumbo!

Fleabus: You are correct that I was referring to 'intrinsic' levels of consciousness rather than 'emergent' consciousness when I claimed that you were no more conscious than a flea.

Jim: So I *am* more conscious than a flea.

Fleabus: If you believe in panpsychist emergence. But I don't.

Jim: Why on earth not?

Fleabus: I feel consciousness. I see consciousness. But I neither see nor feel emergence! Do you?

Jim: I can't say that I have.

The Mysterious Mind

Fleabus: I can see cause-and-effect – when Billiard Ball A hits Billiard Ball B, this causes B to move. But wherever I search I see no emergence.

Jim: Yes!

Fleabus: Nor can I imagine how such a thing could possibly occur. Can you?

Jim: I can't say that I can.

Fleabus: So why postulate such a thing?

Jim: Because I feel superior to a flea!

Fleabus: Exactly.

Jim: So, if there is no emergence then I could be no more conscious than a flea?

Fleabus: That's right. You would be a 'subvenist.'

Jim: Oh! But even if it were true that a flea contained the same level of consciousness as me, surely my experiences of that consciousness would be far greater.

Fleabus: As a 'subvenist' I reject the notion of different *levels* of consciousness between species. But I do agree with you that your *experience* would be different.

Jim: So I *am* more conscious than a flea!

Fleabus: No! Your consciousness is not greater. Talk of levels is meaningless. There is always 'variable expression' in consciousness – there is always a different atomic composition and variable form in every organism. However, this only gives rise to differential experiences because of an 'illusory organismic superstructure.'

Jim: But I am sure that my mind is superior to that of a flea!

Fleabus: Your 'mind' does not exist – what you perceive as your mind is only an 'illusory superstructure' created by the 'supervenience' of your brain on the 'subvenience base' of your atomic consciousness.

Jim: But I am sure that a flea cannot do algebra!

Fleabus: Of course you have superior mental abilities than a flea. But I thought we were talking about consciousness, not your brain.

The Mysterious Mind

Jim: My consciousness is not in my brain!

Fleabus: Of course not. Your consciousness pervades your whole body. Your brain *is* connected to your whole body in order that your actions can be coordinated in a way that maximises your survival chances, but it *isn't* the source of your consciousness.

Jim: I am not sure about that.

Fleabus: Consciousness resides in all atoms, so the brain is simply a conscious part of the body.

Jim: So my brain gives me greater mental capacities but not greater consciousness.

Fleabus: Yes.

Jim: I'm still not sure. I am sure that my depth of experiences is greater than a flea. Can a flea go the opera, appreciate fine art and watch the Simpsons?

Fleabus: Remember we said that consciousness does not emerge. These experiences are a function of your brain.

The Mysterious Mind

Jim: But I am sure that I have feelings that a flea doesn't have. Can a flea love like me?

Fleabus: There could be feelings in a flea that are analogous to your feelings of love. But, love is a complex thing that seems to involve more than feelings.

Jim: So my brain doesn't increase my consciousness?

Fleabus: That's right.

Jim: Okay, so I am not more conscious than a flea.

14. Conclusions

In the first part of the book I reviewed the four most plausible philosophical explanations of consciousness outlined by Koch. I argued that both the materialist and the panpsychist route were possible explanations for consciousness. However, I concluded that the repositioning of the 'hard problem' at the origination of planetary life that is enabled by the philosophy of Jonas, when combined with the arguments concerning the infeasibility of turning an unconscious substance into a conscious substance, make the panpsychist route more believable. I also concluded that some of Dennett's arguments were convincing.

In the second half of the book I have attempted to fuse together the best bits of panpsychism and Dennett into a new paradigm which I have called 'subvenience'. This paradigm is based on the fallacy of organismic consciousness levels, the non-emergence of consciousness from the atomic level, the continuous flux of object boundaries, and the inauthenticity of consciousness that increases with the functional complexity of nervous systems / brains.

The key claim of subvenience is that consciousness is located at the atomic level in a 'subvenience base'. What we generally refer to as consciousness is simply the 'illusory organismic superstructure' that arises in organisms with a nervous system. This superstructure is very similar to the Joycean

Machine of Dennett – the superstructure is simply extended to all entities with nervous systems. However, the presence of the 'subvenience base' which 'subvenes' the brain means that all entities can 'feel'; they can all experience qualia. The important thing is that the continuous flux of object boundaries means that *all* entities comprise a 'universal subvenience base'. Therefore, the experiences of entities without an 'illusory organismic superstructure' will be purely a function of the spatio-temporally embedded atoms. It is on this 'universal base' that the 'illusory organismic experiences' of entities with nervous systems are built. Humans cannot create consciousness because they cannot expand the 'universal subvenience base'; furthermore, all parts of the subvenience base are unique. This means that functionalism is false – machines cannot be created with the same experiences as a human.

So, *is* there the same level of consciousness in a flea as there is in me? In both materialism and panpsychism there is an incomparably higher level of consciousness in me than there is in a flea. In materialism consciousness is produced by the brain and emerges late in the evolution of the planet. In panpsychism atomic consciousness gives rise to 'emergence' which bolsters consciousness in accordance with the functional complexity of the entity. However, in 'subvenience' there is the same level of consciousness in a flea as there is in me. The only difference between us is the higher inauthenticity of illusion that results from my greater 'illusory organismic superstructure'. So, the answer depends on your preferred paradigm.

References

1. Daniel Dennett, *Consciousness Explained*, (London, Penguin Books Ltd, 1993), pp.37-8.

2. Gerald M. Edelman and Guilio Tononi, *Consciousness – How Matter Becomes Imagination*, (Bath, Penguin Group, 2000), p.36.

3. Hans Jonas, *The Phenomenon of Life*, (Illinois, Northwestern University Press, 2001), p.24.

4. Christian de Quincey, *Radical Nature*, (Montpelier, Invisible Cities Press, 2002), p.289.

5. Christian de Quincey, *Radical Nature*, (Montpelier, Invisible Cities Press, 2002), p.46.

6. Christof Koch, *The Quest for Consciousness*, (Colorado, Roberts & Company Publishers, 2004), pp.4-11.

7. Gerald M. Edelman and Guilio Tononi, *Consciousness – How Matter Becomes Imagination*, (Bath, Penguin Group, 2000), p.5.

8. Christof Koch, *The Quest for Consciousness*, (Colorado, Roberts & Company Publishers, 2004), p.10.

9. Christof Koch, *The Quest for Consciousness*, (Colorado, Roberts & Company Publishers, 2004), p.12.

10. Ervin Laszlo, *Science and the Akashic Field*, (Vermont, Inner Traditions, 2004), p.145.

11. Christof Koch, *The Quest for Consciousness*, (Colorado, Roberts & Company Publishers, 2004), p.13.

12. Hans Jonas, *The Phenomenon of Life*, (Illinois, Northwestern University Press, 2001), p.24.

13. Hans Jonas, *The Phenomenon of Life*, (Illinois, Northwestern University Press, 2001), p.xxiii.

14. Hans Jonas, *The Phenomenon of Life*, (Illinois, Northwestern University Press, 2001), p.3.

15. Christian de Quincey, *Radical Nature*, (Montpelier, Invisible Cities Press, 2002), p.91.

16. Ervin Laszlo, *Science and the Akashic Field*, (Vermont, Inner Traditions, 2004), p.147.

17. Hans Jonas, *The Phenomenon of Life*, (Illinois, Northwestern University Press, 2001), pp.3-4.

18. Hans Jonas, *The Phenomenon of Life* (Illinois, Northwestern University Press, 2001), p.4.

19. Colin McGinn, "Can we solve the mind-body problem?", in *Mind*, 98 (1989), p.349.

20. Christian de Quincey, *Radical Nature*, (Montpelier, Invisible Cities Press, 2002), p.46.

21. Christian de Quincey, *Radical Nature*, (Montpelier, Invisible Cities Press, 2002), p.45.

22. Christian de Quincey, *Radical Nature*, (Montpelier, Invisible Cities Press, 2002), p.46.

23. Christian de Quincey, *Radical Nature*, (Montpelier, Invisible Cities Press, 2002), p.47.

24. Christian de Quincey, *Radical Nature*, (Montpelier, Invisible Cities Press, 2002), p.48.

25. Ervin Laszlo, *Science and the Akashic Field*, (Vermont, Inner Traditions, 2004), pp.146-7.

26. David J. Chalmers, *The Conscious Mind*, (Oxford, Oxford University Press, 1996), p.168.

27. David J. Chalmers, *The Conscious Mind*, (Oxford, Oxford University Press, 1996), p.299.

28. Christian de Quincey, *Radical Nature*, (Montpelier, Invisible Cities Press, 2002), p.91.

29. Erwin Schrodinger, *My View of the World*, (London, Cambridge University Press, 1964), p.43.

30. Christian de Quincey, *Radical Nature*, (Montpelier, Invisible Cities Press, 2002), pp.104-5.

31. Christian de Quincey, *Radical Nature*, (Montpelier, Invisible Cities Press, 2002), p.134.

32. Christian de Quincey, *Radical Nature*, (Montpelier, Invisible Cities Press, 2002), pp.194-5.

33. David J. Chalmers, *The Conscious Mind*, (Oxford, Oxford University Press, 1996), p.248.

34. David J. Chalmers, *The Conscious Mind*, (Oxford, Oxford University Press, 1996), p.298.

35. Christian de Quincey, *Radical Nature*, (Montpelier, Invisible Cities Press, 2002), p.183.

36. David J. Chalmers, *The Conscious Mind*, (Oxford, Oxford University Press, 1996), p.154.

37. David J. Chalmers, *The Conscious Mind*, (Oxford, Oxford University Press, 1996), p.154.

38. Christian de Quincey, *Radical Nature*, (Montpelier, Invisible Cities Press, 2002), p.206.

39. Ervin Laszlo, *Science and the Akashic Field*, (Vermont, Inner Traditions, 2004), p.147.

40. Daniel Dennett, *Consciousness Explained*, (London, Penguin Books Ltd, 1993), p.406.

41. Daniel Dennett, *Consciousness Explained*, (London, Penguin Books Ltd, 1993), p.16.

42. Daniel Dennett, *Consciousness Explained*, (London, Penguin Books Ltd, 1993), p.111.

43. Daniel Dennett, *Consciousness Explained*, (London, Penguin Books Ltd, 1993), p.431.

44. Daniel Dennett, *Consciousness Explained*, (London, Penguin Books Ltd, 1993), p.254.

45. Daniel Dennett, *Consciousness Explained*, (London, Penguin Books Ltd, 1993), p.281.

46. Daniel Dennett, *Consciousness Explained*, (London, Penguin Books Ltd, 1993), p.281.

47. Daniel Dennett, *Consciousness Explained*, (London, Penguin Books Ltd, 1993), p.442.

48. Daniel Dennett, *Consciousness Explained*, (London, Penguin Books Ltd, 1993), p.387.

49. Colin McGinn, "Can we solve the mind-body problem?", in *Mind*, 98 (1989), p.366.

50. Daniel Dennett, *Consciousness Explained*, (London, Penguin Books Ltd, 1993), p.171.

51. Karl-Erik Fichtelius and Sverre Sjolander, *Man's Place*, (Norfolk, Lowe & Brydone Ltd, 1973), p.34.

52. Thomas Nagel, "What is it like to be a bat?", in *Philosophical Review* 83 (1971), p.436.

53. Thomas Nagel, "What is it like to be a bat?", in *Philosophical Review* 83 (1971), p.439.

54. Thomas Nagel, "What is it like to be a bat?", in *Philosophical Review* 83 (1971), p.437.

55. Karl-Erik Fichtelius and Sverre Sjolander, *Man's Place*, (Norfolk, Lowe & Brydone Ltd, 1973), p.40.

56. Christian de Quincey, *Radical Nature*, (Montpelier, Invisible Cities Press, 2002), pp.205-6.

57. M. Davies and G. W. Humphreys, *Consciousness*, (Oxford, Basil Blackwell Ltd, 1993), p.9.

58. Cleve Backster, quoted in, Ervin Laszlo, *Science and the Akashic Field*, (Vermont, Inner Traditions, 2004), p.103.

59. Daniel Dennett, *Consciousness Explained*, (London, Penguin Books Ltd, 1993), p.420.

60. David J. Chalmers, *The Conscious Mind*, (Oxford, Oxford University Press, 1996), p.155.

61. David J. Chalmers, *The Conscious Mind*, (Oxford, Oxford University Press, 1996), p.293.

www.ingramcontent.com/pod-product-compliance
Lightning Source LLC
Chambersburg PA
CBHW071520040426
42444CB00008B/1731